A Dar with L...

Bring your heart along with your eyes.
Come dance with me.

Marlene Neumann

ISBN: 978-0-6397-5595-3(print)
978-0-6397-5596-0(e-book)

First printed 2022
Independently published by Marlene Neumann
Marleneneumann.com

What people are saying

"If you are ready to pause, take time to reflect on your life and self, then this book is an ideal way to begin to do so. Put yourself first and begin a delightful journey into self-discovery." Anne

"A very beautiful book, with a wealth of wisdom & authenticity. It is an uplifting and meaningful work of art. Your words touch both heart & mind, & encompass wonderfully the trials & tribulations we must endure to try to survive at least partly intact." Carol

"You certainly bared your soul with no holding back. I felt your pain on so many levels. I felt as if I was seeing you for the first time. I felt your raw emotions so beautifully written. I went through your hurt with you personally. Thank you for allowing us into your world." Gerry

Seascape I

Why this book now ?

What if our purpose as humans is to dance to nature's rhythm, to soar like eagles and to truly experience everything that life brings us? What if we are meant to learn how to move, sway and when to stay still to navigate our life path rather than hide, or to sit certain dances out?

Life is sometimes slow and steady, other times rocky and uncomfortable. It may seem as if we are going through rapids and feeling as if we will never get out of the cycle that we find ourselves in; being bashed against the rocks of the whirlpool with no place to grab onto to take a breath. Then there are those times life feels as if it's there for us to ride gracefully; like a dolphin joyously dancing in and out of the waves with no effort, having fun with every swoop and dive.

Our lives flow through cycles which are as natural as the seasons. Yet we're not given a map, or even a guide, at birth. We learn from our experiences. We learn from our families, friends and teachers. We gather knowledge and information from our cultures, religions and the societies in which we live. We pick up tips, ideas and rules, mainly unconsciously, and expect to know the best way to live our lives. We don't know what we don't know, and from my own experience of the dance with life, we know very little about ourselves and the world in which we live.

As a child, I was never taught how to dance through my own life, but I learnt, as others do, the hard way - by watching my dearest Mother suffer through her emotions. Yet, I've learnt how to stay on my feet even in the most terrible of life's storms. I've taught thousands of students to learn how to dance through their lives during my 40 years of teaching.

After the last few years of world storms, the time was right to share my life through my images and some of the stories they tell to help more people learn to dance with life. So many have felt alone, abandoned and abused these past few years. Nature too is showing us that she feels that abuse.

Nature is such a wonderful and magical teacher and shows us love through every season that comes around. Nature loves us unconditionally, which I've been fortunate to capture through my photographs for most of my life.

To live fully is to know you have loved those around you and know you have been true to your heart. To know that you have danced and loved fully even when your heart is breaking. To know that you never played it safe.

This book is the story of how I dance with life – waltzing now, fox trotting or doing hip-hop on another day, and sometimes just sitting out, watching others dance. The images in the book reflect the various insights nature has shown me as I've danced with life.

I believe profoundly that we are all one. In our essence, I am a part of you and you are a part of me. The things that we think separate us, are illusions and, very often, delusions. Our inner dance is the process of ridding ourselves of them.

So, in that sense of connectedness and unity, the images and thoughts in this book reflect not just parts of me but also parts of you. The ways in which you respond to them will reflect your dance with life, too.

I hope you enjoy these reflections on my dance and look forward to hearing about your dance with life...

Marlene x
December 2022

A Tribute

I dedicate this book to my dearest sister, Jenny, whom I loved so deeply.

I treasure the gifts you left with me. The most important was the knowledge that we leave this life with absolutely nothing that we accumulated - except the love or lack of it in our hearts.
Your death lifted the veil and allowed me to see more clearly.

To all the township dogs that I spent months getting to know and helping: you are courageous beyond belief. I fully understand why the word 'dog' spelt backwards is no coincidence.

Foreward

I am greatly honoured to have been asked to provide a foreward
to *A Dance with Life*. Both in imagery and text, it is a beautiful and
spiritual book. It is food for the soul: the very sustenance needed
by so many living ego-driven lives, bemused and monopolised by
the material world.

Marlene escorts us away from the restricted confines and 'suffering'
of our 'boxed' city lives into a world of singular beauty and invites
us to let go – let be – and surrender to a beneficent, bountiful and
loving existence and to dance to its rhythm with trust, freedom and
joy. She does so with the humility of a fellow soul, traversing the
same spiritual path, who has herself, like so many, experienced illness, doubt, loss, grief and unrequited love, but has never lost sight
of the ineffable grandeur and magnificence of the Creation, whether
in vast or miniature form.

Against the backdrop of a world fraught with turbulence, conflict,
and pain, she pauses life with her camera and with reverence ad-
dresses the captured image, recognising it as a portal to something
beyond itself, something that would otherwise remain hidden, unknown and indefinable. Without changing the image, she reaches
into the spiritual realm that informs and energises it, senses the
meaning of its ethereal counterpart, and reveals the mysterious
and mystical archetypal world with which it is confluent. Viewing
Marlene's images from the 'un-mind', egoless perspective, we are
in the presence of their invisible essence, which transports us to a
timeless dimension of which they are the epiphany: a dimension
free of chaos and confusion.

Contemplation of Marlene's highly-personal, individualised photographic art-form is therapeutic; it gently persuades the viewer away from an ego-based to a soul-based perspective – relieving the psyche at the deepest level possible: the soul dimension.

Her autobiographical reflections are in perfect keeping with the images that support and illustrate them and are studded with philosophical gems and inspirational insights, affording direction to those similarly distressed by the vagaries and challenges of life. Knowing her and the events of her life well, I am deeply moved by the sincerity and openness with which she communicates her message based upon the solid rock of her life experience and the caring work she is doing with township dogs. Marlene embodies her teaching and gives it expression through her words and the loving tenderness of her very special photographic art.

David Lilley – author of *Healing the Soul*

World renowned homeopathic doctor, author, teacher, mentor

Contents

List of Images

My Law - Tieme Tanapiri

A Maori Poem

The sun may be clouded, yet ever the sun
Will sweep on its course 'till the Cycle is run.
And when into chaos the system is hurled
Again shall the Builder reshape a new world.
Your path may be clouded, uncertain your goal:
Move on - for your orbit is fixed to your soul.
And though it may lead into darkness of night,
The torch of the Builder shall give it new light.
You were. You will be. Know this while you are:
Your spirit has travelled both long and afar.

It came from the Source, to the Source it returns -
The Spark which was lighted eternally burns.
It slept in a jewel. It leapt in a wave.
It roamed in the forest. It rose from the grave.
It took on strange garbs for long aeons of years,
And now in the soul of yourself It appears.
From body to body your spirit speeds on,
It seeks a new form when the old one has gone.
And the form that it finds is the fabric you wrought
On the loom of the Mind from the fibre of Thought.

As dew is drawn upwards, in rain to descend,
Your thoughts drift away and in Destiny blend.
You cannot escape them, for petty or great,
Or evil or noble, they fashion your Fate.
Somewhere on some planet, sometime and somehow,
Your life will reflect your thoughts of your Now.
My Law is unerring, no blood can atone -
The structure you built you will live in - alone.
From Cycle to Cycle, through time and through space,
Your lives with your longings will ever keep pace,

And all that you ask for, and all you desire,
Must come at your bidding, as flame out of fire.
Once list' to that Voice and all tumult is done -
Your life is the life of the Infinite One.
In the hurrying race you are conscious of pause,
With love for the purpose, and love for the Cause.
You are your own Devil, you are your own God,
You fashioned the paths your footsteps have trod.
And no one can save you from Error or Sin
Until you have hark'd to the Spirit within.

Oyster Catchers

The Search

My life experience has taught me that we are all searching.
A search for a partner, the best career, the most wonderful house.
For happiness.

I've always been a seeker, just like anyone else. I was striving to prove myself by attaining status, wealth and numerous relation-ships to find fulfilment in my life. We all ask: Which way should I go? What road shall I choose? We are always looking to others to fulfil a deep need inside of ourselves. There's much talk of "mid-life crisis," which to my mind is simply a deep part of ourselves want-ing to find that part of ourself which we feel is missing.

Yet, it is simply the act of knowing ourselves that brings us serenity, calm and contentment. It's ultimately our own inner peace that we're seeking in life. We're simply unaware of that as our schooling doesn't teach that we already have everything we need to dance through life. If only we'd listened to the wise words, "Know thyself," we'd have found peace much sooner.

Finding the sweet spot in which we can find our path back to our true home inside of ourselves brings us contentment and peace. Yet we choose to have an inner struggle with ourselves to try to stay in control, believing that's what society has taught us to do. By allowing our dance to be controlled by external events and other people we are in fact not listening to that part of ourselves which knows how to balance everything so we can dance through life with love and joy.

The two images in this chapter, *Oyster Catchers* and *As Above So Below*, show us that we must surrender to something higher and deeper than us. Trust the universe. Trust God. Trust life. Know,

As Above So Below

understand, accept that we actually have no control and that it's right that we don't. Each of us is about the size of a grain of sand in the bigger scheme of things in the world.

We may feel as if we're on the edge of change in every moment, just as the tide and the waves create a changing scene in every second. In many ways we are on the edge of change. We can choose to go forwards, backwards, sideways or stand still. We can choose to sit down. We can even choose to bury our heads in the sand. Whether we like it or not, the world around us changes in every fraction of a second. We can choose to dance with the change or try to resist it.

My Dad had a heart attack and died right in front of me when I was just 17 years old. In that moment my life changed. The tide had turned for me in a blink of an eye. One heart stopped beating which altered the course of many other hearts. I had no choice about the change, but I could choose what my next step in life would be. My Mom was distraught. My sisters were already married and had left home, so I was left to care for Mom, feeling every tear she shed and all the sadness she felt. I took on the responsibility of the family home; looking after everyone despite not feeling this was my job, or skill set, in life.

Even though I'd felt Dad was absent from my everyday upbringing, this instant change in circumstance rocked my world to the core and changed the direction of my life. Instead of going away to Teacher Training College, I stayed close by, living with Mom as I studied art and design locally and creating my career from this new starting point.

I don't regret any choices I've made in my life. I've learnt to live with the decisions I've made. I've made some tough decisions. I've defied doctors. I've gone against expert advice; as I've followed my inner guidance in many situations. It's never been easy. I've laughed and cried. I've ranted to God. Yet, I've learnt to dance so many different steps that I feel free to be myself, living my life in the very best way for me. I've found a way, knowing myself in the deepest way possible, to dance to my own rhythm. We must understand that we get what we need in life and not what we want.

I've learnt that we create many illusions in our minds, especially when we're feeling as if we're living in chaos and confusion. In our hearts, everything is calm and clear. This may just sound like words on paper, but I'm speaking from deep and repeated personal experience. Whenever I've been 'in flow', surrendered to the moment and let go of trying to control things, a sense of stillness comes over me. That's learning to dance to the rhythm of life, hearing the ups-and-downs in the music and changing my direction, steps and sometimes partners accordingly.

The two images, *Oyster Catchers* and *As Above So Below*, are so different. You wouldn't expect one photographer to capture both. But they reflect a profound reality. Through severe life experiences I have come to understand inner serenity in the same way I understand chaos and emotional confusion. I know the craziness of nothing being like it used to be, or like I expect it to be. I know what it feels like to be indecisive, not understanding which is the right path to take. There is a balancing act that we embark on when we enter the realm of confusion. It should be exciting, but it is also unsettling and scary.

Just like any adventure, we experience the whole range of emotions.

When I capture the spirit of nature in my photographic images, I am reminded that deep inside me there is no confusion, no anxiety. I drop into a place of centeredness, a place where I have no-mind; a place where I'm simply connected to myself, which in turn connects me to everything around me.

The part of me that captures the photograph instinctively recognises, connects and loves spirit, energy, harmony – the flow of life. It knows what I must do and how to do it. I'm simply following my inner guidance to press the shutter at that millisecond in time to frame what the eye doesn't always see but the heart knows.

In each chapter I will share with you some of my black-and-white images and the connection I made to the world around me from the point in life I was at in that moment in time. I encourage you to be open to explore the images you see and the words you hear as you turn each page and immerse yourself in this dance with life.

Dune Grass

Taking the first step

I find you can tell a great deal about a photographer based on the images he or she takes.

I remain as intrigued by black-and-white photography today as I was when I was 14 years old and introduced to the darkroom when I started taking photographs at school.

In all that time, the same thread – spirit - has run through my images. That said, as we all do, I have grown emotionally and spiritually throughout my life. My life has been quite a journey, sometimes extremely challenging. Throughout my dance through life, I have observed that when my internal world expanded the things I saw outside of myself changed and the depth of my images increased.

My continuous search for truth has influenced my work deeply. My entire life is, and has been, a devotion to finding the path home to the divine. One of the most vital discoveries on that journey has been the discovery that the path is within each of us. All the striving I was doing was in the (outer) world I was living in, instead of turning my attention inwards to myself. This world we are living in now with technology and social media has created more distractions to stop us from connecting to ourselves. When you search outside of yourself it can derail you and take you longer to get back on to your own personal path. My knowledge has come from deep within myself as I have learnt how to connect to my highest truth.

Our true self is a concept that you may or may not be familiar with, but it's still the right one. Who am I? What is my real purpose? Those questions echo down the millennia and across every expression of human activity. Yet, so few humans set out to find out who they truly are. It's in this search to find my true self that I continue my personal journey of discovery, to seek out every part of me through all my experiences through life.

Over the years, as I've taught photography and interacted with people who have bought my images, I've spoken to literally thousands of people. Without exception, everyone is struggling with a disconnection from themselves. Most people manage to numb the pain with alcohol or other interests that distract them from the real issue - themselves. They just won't go there, to themselves.

Whenever I have the opportunity, I make a point of chatting to people about how they feel; what is their connection to God and their spirit. I don't mean this in the context of any religion but through your authentic self. Who are you really? People don't like to talk much about feelings. Men, in particular, shy away from the subject. Yet, how we feel is important. It matters. We need to tune into our feelings every day. Working with our emotions is what will guide us back to our true selves.

I have been fortunate in this life, as I have been able to capture the beauty of Nature, my images helping me to work through the struggles of life. They have been the stepping stones to my personal inner reality. The process of capturing them is continually teaching me who I really am. I am not just a photographer. I am much more than that. I am spirit.

When I capture the images, I drop into a space that is like being underwater. It is incredibly silent. It is as though I die to the material world and awake into one of spiritual energy. I don't have to go anywhere or do anything. I simply am.

It would be wonderful to live my entire life from that space of harmony and serenity. But, when you're underwater, you have to come up periodically for air. You do have to function in the physical world, finding the balance between the silence and the noise. Living in silence amidst the noise is the skill I am continually developing.

I feel like a caterpillar that has been wrapped in its cocoon, but can now see a hole in the cocoon. I see a new existence waiting for me, as a butterfly; as a whole, complete being, free to be me.

My black-and-white work is the hole in the cocoon, for me. And it tells everyone who views it that there is something out there for them. We all have our strengths and weaknesses. Working with them gently and lovingly is what helps the caterpillar leave the cocoon and become the butterfly.

Grass Pods

No Mind

There came a time, some years ago, when the person I'd been was not working for me. I felt uncomfortable in my skin, as though I didn't fit it anymore. I sensed that I was not connected to a reality that mattered. At the same time, I couldn't figure out what the reality I was missing looked or felt like.

Slowly, I realised that, in fact, I had always known what mattered. Instinctively, when I took photographs, I entered a place of knowing my true self, who I am deep in my core. Because it was instinctive, I took it for granted and never analysed or articulated what I was doing.

The more time I spent out of that place of being myself, the more I felt out of sorts. The discomfort forced me to examine why I was suffocating, trapped in the cocoon of unawareness that I had created in order to succeed in what society had made me think was the real world.

I began to understand that when I was 'in my mind,' thinking about things, I was away from my centre, my being, my Self. When I let go of my mind, I was where I needed to be. You can see when you look into people's eyes that they are trapped in a mental landscape of intellect.

There is a difference between working from the mind instead of experiencing life through the connection directly to your heart. It's difficult to put into words – because it's a place where words are irrelevant. So, let me use a practical example:

A feral cat started visiting my home, looking for the food I left out for her. I had built enough trust with her for her to come into the house and, sometimes, sit on the couch within my reach. But she would never let me touch her.

One day, sitting with her, I went into the no-mind, my underwater state from which I take photographs. In the silence there, she and I felt the same. I felt like I was a cat. I reached over and touched her gently under her chin and on her tummy. For about three minutes, we communicated at the level of universal energy where beings are not separate. Then, I changed. I began to wonder how long I could go on without surfacing into my mind. Of course, by wondering, I had already surfaced into my mind. She jumped up immediately and went outside.

My work, every day, is to intentionally take my awareness 'under-water'; to bring what I do instinctively in taking photographs into my day-to-day existence, so that I can tap into essence all of the time; so that the whole of my life is about essence and not just those moments when I am taking a photograph.

I am focusing on consciously stepping through the veil, which is my busy mind, that separates me from my reality. Transforming my pain into deep self-realisation helps me to understand who I am, what has formed and shaped me and how I can use my life experiences as a stepping stone to God realisation.

Structure keeps us stuck

I believe that we're born in a state of no-mind. Babies are in direct contact with their emotions. There's no difference between who they are inside themselves and the way they express themselves to the outer world.

As we grow, in kicks the system. People tend to roll their eyes when I talk about the 'system' because I sound like a conspiracy theorist.

Whether or not there is a proactive conspiracy by a group of people trying to control the world isn't relevant. What does matter is that society is constructed according to the mind and the intellect and, in that system of being, information becomes a tool that keeps us from understanding that we are beings of light having a human experience.

So... when you're at school, the more accurately you can learn someone else's material and regurgitate it, the more prizes you win and the cleverer you feel. If you're not strong academically, you can excel in sport, where the process of winning and losing traps you into a different delusion of success.

We never question the underlying concepts. What we end up with is a mind in which stale useless thoughts buzz around relentlessly, like flies. We deny ourselves the ability to see all those invisible things beyond the mind that cannot be seen with the naked eye.

One of those things is energy - universal and personal. Some of the others are emotions. The ones we lose altogether are love and compassion, not just for others but also ourselves. Instead, we judge others and ourselves. "This is right. That's wrong."

Water Lillies

Yet, without really knowing what the pain is inside us, we yearn to get back to that inner child who lived knowing unconditional love for themselves and everything around them. Subconsciously, the way we present ourselves to the world today reflects how that child was treated.

In all the photography and creativity workshops I've presented over the years, I've seen hundreds of adults who pride themselves on their intellectual, analytical, mind-based abilities. Yet, they cannot cope in my world of being free to connect with nature and the creativity that allows us.

They've done well in the system, prospering materially and becoming role models for the next generation. But the ache for something more is still there. They think they've come on a photographic workshop. In fact, they've come in search of themselves, because creativity is a direct connection to the divine part of each of us. Yet, it is the one aspect of the schooling system that has virtually been removed. As a result, we find children growing up stunted and frustrated and adults who are blocked and detached from themselves and others.

The system has failed them with regards to the most important aspect of their existence. Something guides them to come to my workshops rather than others, because, although they don't know it, I will get them to explore emotions, energy, spirit.

Albert Einstein said: "Everyone is a genius. But if you judge a fish on its ability to climb a tree, it will live its whole life believing that it is stupid."

In the absence of a school and social system that looks at you as you are and helps you make the best of your particular strengths, you have to find your own way back to your true self.

Desertscape

Listening without Ears,
Seeing without Eyes

The word tenebrosity helped me one day to understand that part of our difficulty in rediscovering the innocence with which we arrive in life as babies, and lose as the system closes in around us, is the fact that we don't know what we don't know.

We don't know – or we forget – that there is an inner world of emotion, energy, and spirit that is our true home as humans. It's the only reality. The external world is simply a construct of the mind. If you challenge it, it vanishes.

I can feel your doubt.

But, let the logic unfold. Just for this moment, put all your preconceived ideas about the world and yourself to one side. They'll be waiting for you if you really want them back...

We think there's no inner world because we think we have not experienced it. Like the members of the audience of a motivational speaker who said when asked, that they couldn't imagine tenebrosity because they didn't know what it was. When the speaker told them tenebrosity is the quality of being dark or shadowy, they realised they all knew what darkness and shadow looked like. So, in fact, they absolutely could imagine tenebrosity.

All we need to do, to connect with spirit, energy, self, is to open ourselves to the possibility that we already know what that is. Katy, the feral cat whom you met 'underwater' earlier in the book, has never lived inside a house. So, when she visits me, she is fascinated by the way the floor mats skid on the tiles, the way my fingers wiggle when I want to attract her attention, the smell and structure of a piece of rice when I put it in her food bowl. She's willing to explore new concepts.

Daisies

In the same way, we all need to remind ourselves that we already interact with the world of spirit and energy in every minute of our day. More than that, our existence depends on it. All we need to do is be willing to explore it. Energy streams at us all the time. It comes from a leaf, a stone, a bone, a face, the sky. It's inseparable from who we are, even if we're unaware of this in our conscious existence from moment to moment.

I've been given the gift of being able to capture energy through my camera lens. It streams out of my images because I am open to it, and I align my entire body and being with it. I don't look at things with my mind. I feel things with my heart. When there's resonance between me and the subject, the photograph takes itself. Often, I see the image inside myself just before I click the shutter. It has its own existence and it tells me that it's there.

Remember that everything in the world existed before our system gave it a name. It will continue to exist long after all of the names for it in all the different languages of the world have faded into history.

The Latin word for 'tree' was 'arbor'. But no-one speaks Latin anymore. The word has disappeared from daily use. The English word 'tree' will also disappear one day. But trees will remain.

The strangeness of that thought should help us remember that the world of words, information, concepts – in other words, the mind – is temporary. We can't rely on it to help us find ourselves.

Life really is like a dance, taking two steps this way and one step that way. We never quite know where it will take us. Over time, I've realised that everything will pass. But, when it's all happening, you have to ride the waves. You have to take the plunge and make it work. When you're in the lull of the wave, you have to remember that that's ok, too. We cannot have only one side to life. This world is a balance of all things. Nothing is ever missing from our lives. This is difficult to understand when you are experiencing a crisis. But we are always supported, even when we feel alone.

Human behaviour specialist, Dr John Demartini confirms through his work that everything has benefits and drawbacks. He teaches that we have to have balance in mind, body and spirit to be able to keep dancing through life. What happens is we become polarized by only seeing one side of something and this is when we suffer.

If we only believe something is all good, we will eventually hit a barrier, as life has both yin and yang in everything. Having this understanding has helped me a great deal. We become infatuated with things, a situation, or people and later on we find they have disappointed us. The thing that disappointed us was in fact always there. We just chose not to see it. It's like we're living with blinkers on.

Once I learned the lesson and practised awareness of it, I found that I no longer have many highs. You may say that's depressing, but there's a reason highly evolved people have a permanent smile. They know that true happiness comes from the ability to stay calm in the eye of the storm.

As the Buddha said: 'Let us rise up and be thankful, for if we didn't learn a lot, at least we learned a little and if we didn't learn a little, at least we didn't get sick, and if we got sick, at least we didn't die; so, let us all be thankful.'

In my life, this approach has translated into finding and living as much as possible in no-mind. It means discovering what we don't know. It means hearing without our physical ears; seeing without our physical eyes. It means hearing the beat of life underneath all of the external noise of living.

Ancient Wisdom

Words are tools of the mind. So, they are flawed. They are not absolutes. They can easily be misinterpreted.

So, as I write about no-mind here, I am aware that the words I'm using are not in themselves the experiences I have had or the ones you could have. They are simply descriptions of the experiences. As a result, their usefulness to you may be limited. My images, on the other hand, do enable you to have the experience I had when I took the photos. There is an immediate transfer from the image to the viewer of the no-mind moment that was captured when the shutter clicked.

Why is that?

When I had taken the image *Serene Tree*, which has an extraordinary Zen energy, I felt that I had achieved the ultimate expression of its essence. I didn't believe I could go further. But, one day, I was sitting alone at one of my favourite places – the beach. I was eating some homemade sandwiches and surrendering utterly to my love of the sea in particular, and life in general. Being alone, my feeling of being connected to the Source and life was very strong. I felt that I had come home. Not to the beach, but to my Self.

I strolled a bit further, feeling that I was in love, that I could see the hole in the cocoon through which my butterfly self would emerge. I saw the ibises at the edge of the water and wanted to photograph them, but was distracted when some dogs ran up to greet me. The moment for the Ibis image had not arrived.

The dog's owner came over to chat. I was a little resistant, thinking that I would lose my connection to the energy of the ibises.

Sacred Ibis

Because I didn't want to be rude, I agreed to walk with my newly met companion to her house to meet her bedridden mother.

As we turned to go to the house, the dogs ran ahead of us, causing the ibises to take to the air. And, before I knew it, the camera was at my eye and the shutter was clicking. I took three photos in split seconds, not stopping to check f-stops or any other technical details.

I've not had to crop or adjust the image that you see on this page. The exposure and composition are exactly as they should be because, in spite of having unexpected and unfamiliar company, I was still steeped in the energy and essence of the moment.

I now know that this is the way I should live every moment: rooted in essence, love, connected to my source energy, while interacting with the external facets of the world with love and kindness. If you like, interacting directly from my soul with the external world. That way, only love and kindness is possible.

When I met my companion's mother, expecting to be disturbed by her bedridden circumstances, I found a woman whose face had the bright cheerfulness of a sunflower. She shone, inside and out. Her window looked straight out onto the beach and gave her an unlimited view of the ever-changing beauty of the sea. She found great joy in that. Or maybe she knew she was returning to that.

I was given two gifts that day. One was the Sacred Ibis image. The other was an insight into grace in challenging circumstances.

Had I not been in no-mind at the time, the ancient wisdom that underlies all of life and expresses itself as love could not have reached me.

And I could not have paid it forward through my image.

Serene Tree

It's OK to be vulnerable

I talk a great deal in my work with students of life, about being open and vulnerable, and so allowing life to reach you where you are at any moment in time.

 That's because essence, energy, spirit won't make itself visible if you're distracted, busy, angry, or full of ego. It waits for you to be receptive.

What does being receptive really mean?

At a personal level, having always been extremely sensitive, I've inherently been receptive to other people's feelings. Remember, everything has benefits and drawbacks. For me, sensing others' feelings has created an immense sense of vulnerability. My personal boundaries have felt extremely porous. So, I've been open but also vulnerable. As an artist, this can be a blessing or a curse.

I'm not the exception though. For everyone in the midst of the hustle-and-bustle of life, being open to feelings, whether they are your own or someone else's, brings discomfort initially. It means being soft, gentle, and, inevitably, vulnerable. Yet, the gentleness, the vulnerability is at the core of everything. It's what ties living beings – and even things like rocks, water, and the air – together, into wholeness.

Being open means operating at a soul level.

Imagine if we could all deal with one another on a soul level. How different, how tender life would be! That's not really possible, of course, until each of us develops the ability to deal with ourselves on a soul level. As I now understand it, that means making an

Dewdrops II

appointment with yourself, every day. Being alone with yourself. It's so easy to do. You're alone with yourself the moment you close your eyes. You're alone with yourself the moment you connect consciously with your breath. In those moments, we begin to strip away the veil that separates us from true reality, from everything we cannot see with the naked eye. We move closer to the truth. What is the 'truth'? After years of searching for the answer, I have learned that it is whatever is left after we drop all of our ideas, beliefs or concepts. Finding the truth is not about acquiring something. It's about letting go of everything. It's about releasing everything that you thought you were. It's about understanding that we are not here forever. That in itself should make us all have the realization that we are merely passing through this life.

The truth is about letting go of fear and judgement. It's about realising that we are not separate from others or the world. We all struggle with the same things and in the same way. Even people who have excelled within the system that I talked about earlier are in the same boat, searching for a truth that doesn't exist within the system of society as we've come to know it.

Even when we've accumulated a lot of knowledge and education, we are severely handicapped when it comes to handling or controlling our own emotions.

I remember some of my emotional blockages crumbling when I read Don Miguel Ruiz's little book, *The Four Agreements*. The agreements are amazingly simple, yet have changed me in an incredible way.

Dewdrops IV

He suggests that you agree with your self to: (1) Be Impeccable with your word; speak (and think), with integrity (2) Don't take anything personally (3) Don't make assumptions (4) Always do your best.

So much of the way I interact with people and the way they respond to me changed positively after I put each of the four agreements into practice. I literally practiced them for months until they became second nature, especially the one that refers to taking things personally. We make it all about us, don't we? Other people's actions hurt us because we make it about us. This was truly life changing for me.

When I thought back on what the agreements had taught me, I realised they were based in love. Love is ultimately all we are and the only thing to which we return.

The truth always shows itself in the essence, energy, spirit – love. And it's the same love that streams out of my images. Not because I am a particularly gifted photographer. But because, from child-hood, I've somehow been receptive to those things that cannot be seen by the naked eye; to the universal truth that is in all of us and that we all share. So, my images are an encouragement for others to be open, vulnerable – and to truly be alive, to make your life count. To make it real for you; when you don't take things personally you start living for yourself and not through others.

It's OK to show yourself to others. There is no need to wear a mask, put up a barrier or hide who you are. It's OK to feel scared, just like the child you once were. Only when you are openly your-self, accepting all of those parts of you that have made you you, will others openly show themselves to you. Showing vulnerability is not a weakness. It simply allows you to dance to your own rhythm through life without tripping yourself up.

Succulent I

You are the most important person in your life

We spend our whole lives searching for things outside of us to complete us, or make us happy, whereas all we need is to connect to what's inside of us.

How many people pop in and out of our lives on a daily basis, robbing us of our energy and peace? Are they the ones who should be important in our lives? How many people bring harmony to our days? If one were truthful, extremely few.

Should these few take precedence in our lives? Do they outweigh the attention and nurturing we should give ourselves but so rarely do?

I asked myself this question when I went off for three days to a Buddhist retreat centre. It had been a very difficult year in which I twice experienced deep grief – for very different reasons. I had unexpectedly lost a sister to an illness no-one has yet defined. We had very little indication that she was so profoundly ill. In addition, one of my staff members, who had been with me for almost two decades and had become an integral part of the business as I then understood it to be, had left.

Finding my equilibrium again after both losses and redefining my business with new people and the different energy they brought in was extremely challenging. At the same time, I was having to come to terms with the extreme poverty in the townships to which black South Africans had been confined during the Apartheid years. More than two decades after the country's miraculously peaceful transition to democracy, the majority of black South Africans still live in these enclaves, confronting an immense daily struggle for existence.

Succulent II

On a weekly basis, I was going into the townships with my team of volunteers from the Buckaroo sterilization project. Through this project I had founded many years ago through my love and connection to animals, I witnessed for myself the suffering of people and animals.

You can imagine, then, just how physically and emotionally exhausted I was from these internal and external challenges I was experiencing, as I embarked on my retreat.

All of us strive to be positive, but the reality of life is that we all do hit bumps. An equal and very interesting reality is that our darkest times are the ones that make us grow. As Buddhist teacher and psychologist, Jack Kornfield, says, "Our difficulties are our path."

Because of this perspective on the down times, I've learned to love the term 'our shadow self'. We all have one. I spent a great deal of time trying to hide mine; until I realised that we have to reveal both the light and shadow sides of ourselves or the very thing we're trying to hide will eventually show its ugly head. It has to come out sometime and will often show itself to the outside world in the form of an illness which, stuck in our conventional mindsets, will suppress the symptoms that are wanting to be looked at.

For example, I have times when my head and my heart are in conflict and I end up with a stiffness in my neck and shoulders. If I take a pain relief tablet I'm not dealing with the tension which is showing itself for me to deal with. Just as Louise Hay says, "When we create peace and harmony in our minds, we will find it in our lives. No matter where we have come from, we can change our lives for the better."

I knew, when I started my retreat, that the shadow I'd suppressed all of my life needed some attention. It was what was making me so tired. Throughout my life, I've overcome crises by spending time on my own. As an introvert, I am easily drained by being around people all the time and I can revive myself only by being on my own. Most people struggle with solitude. I can understand that, especially if you are an extrovert and you need to be stimulated. For me, being alone is a survival mechanism.

On the first night at the retreat, even though I was desperate for the silence and solitude, I had to watch myself struggling to quiet my mind. I couldn't find the underwater, no-mind place from which I take my photographs. Instead, I was hyper-aware of a rain bird calling in the surrounding forest. Of the frogs. The insects. The laughing, shouting, loud music, and hurly burly of life in the township that borders the retreat.

I was in a retreat but I was still not out of the world, by myself.

I went out for a walk the next day, hoping that nature would calm me, as it normally does. But one of the other people at the retreat wanted to walk with me, chatting merrily. I felt my energy draining away. Sometimes the dance with life is just one twirl two many.

The dance also has a way of restoring balance. A day later, when the stress I was carrying made my hips unbearably stiff and sore, the person who was so insistent on chatting to me turned out to be a practitioner of accupressure. Under the trees, with me lying on the grass in tears of pain and gratitude, she probed and released the knots of distress and exhaustion.

Looking back, I realised that, by going to the retreat centre, by booking a healing appointment with myself, by making myself, just for those three days, the most important person in my life, I had opened the door to healing.

My 700 km journey had taken me to a person who could offer me the healing I needed. And, by being kind and patient, in spite of my screaming nerves wanting to reject the idea of someone walking with me, I had created the opportunity for kindness and love to be offered to me.

Have you ever noticed how dances tend to work in circles? In the dance with life, you always come back to yourself. Pay attention to yourself. You're the most important person you will ever know.

A Winter morning

Boxed in

As I returned from the retreat centre, trying to integrate the peace I had found with all the activity of day-to-day life in the airport, on the roads, in my office, I realised how we live in boxes.

We wake up in a box, which is our bedroom. We shower in a box called a bathroom. We eat breakfast in a box called a dining room or the kitchen. Then we go to the box called the garage and get into the box called the car. We spend our day in a box called the office and then we reverse the process of travelling in the car box back to our home box and end the day sleeping in our bedroom box.

At the retreat, I had spent some time watching the pulse in my arm. We so seldom look at what's underneath or inside anything; what's inside our bodies, our box existences, our minds, our lives. We live on the surface. Our day-to-day activities are inherently superficial.

As I like to say, we live above our shoulders – in the mind.

Small wonder that we constantly feel the need for something more. We look for it outside, of course - in relationships, movies, sport, work, things.

But, if the 'more' were to be found in those things, we'd all have found it by now.

Strange that we don't see our lack of logic in looking in the same places over and over again for what, clearly, cannot be found there! You may be familiar with the saying, "If you do what you've always done, you'll get what you always got".

The Gates

If you do ask for help, expect all hell to break loose

I have a life-threatening illness in my late thirties to thank for kick-starting me on my journey to re-connect with my true self. It made me realise that, although I had ticked most of the boxes by which the system measures material success, I had none of the answers to the big questions of: Why Me? What's Life All About? and What is Death?

I went on more self-help courses and workshops than you can imagine. I read one self-help and spiritually inspirational book after the other.

I found a great deal of useful information – and a significant amount of emotional support. It's wonderful to know that there are people out there who have struggled as you are doing and have found ways to process the struggle.

The process reminded me of the beautiful story of Alice In Wonderland. I can so relate to falling down the rabbit hole. Most of us see discovering ourselves, going down the rabbit hole of "finding yourself," as a huge risk. We don't see it as the adventure it actually is. Yes, you run screaming, even from yourself. But, if you pay attention when you're screaming, you realise there is absolutely nowhere to go but within yourself.

What no-one warned me about, though, was that the journey towards yourself is a journey of constant change. You're peeling off layer after layer of thickly encrusted but entirely useless ideas, opinions, concepts, and expectations. Each time you do that, you bleed a little. You have to wait for scars to heal. You have to start again with the world – and yourself - in a new way.

So, by asking for answers, you're actually asking for change. And when you change, all hell breaks loose – because nothing is the same. Or, nothing is the way you expected it to be.

I know now that change doesn't come with a hammock. You can't embark on a spiritual journey and say: 'I don't want the difficult bits. This bit doesn't suit me. Make it easier. Make it more fun.'

The good news is that struggling pretty much guarantees that you will eventually reach the core, your essence, your true self. The struggle is, in fact, the point. Specifically, the way you struggle is the point.

I used to think I had it all together. Then I stopped and asked myself: What exactly is 'together'? After all the changes I've been through and am still going through, I now believe that having it all together means having the deep persistence and perseverance to shine. Shine under all circumstances. Not just in times of success.

It's only when you reach the bottom of the barrel that you see there in the dregs a true reflection of who you are.

That's when you are forced, through exhaustion on all levels, to just sit quietly with yourself.

That's when you realise that we're all together, all the same in our search for meaning. And... that each one of us is also totally on our own in that search. Because the search is inside yourself, not out there with everyone else.

It was at the bottom of the barrel one day, after all of the books, courses, and workshops trying to find my purpose and the meaning of my life, that I realised that whatever it is I'm doing or am right now is already it. I'm where I need to be, doing what I need to be doing.

But, instead of being and doing it blindly, I'm aware. I know how to find meaning in it.

> "It may be when we no longer know what to do,
> we have come to our real work,
> and that when we no longer know which way to go,
> we have begun our real journey,
> The mind that is not baffled is not employed.
> The impeded stream is the one that sings."
> Wendell Berry, from <u>Standing by Words</u>

This is the reason why I tell the attendees at my creativity workshops: Unleash whatever you feel inside you. Who cares if someone says it is 'right' or 'wrong'? There is, in fact, no 'right' or 'wrong'. There is only what's left when you get rid of concepts like right and wrong. Let go of who you thought you were. We made up our identity anyway.

The Boat

Everything is a mirror

The image of *The Boat* on this page took me six months to complete. That surprises many people, who think that the work is over once the shutter has clicked.

In 40 years, I've never cropped an image of my own. Like the old masters of the 1940s, I believe you cannot make a photograph after you have taken it. It must just be there. In any case, it's an old master skill - being able to take exactly what you see and feel. That's what separates photographs from fine art images. As I've said earlier in this book, I 'see' the image in my soul a split second before I take it. More accurately, the image shows itself to me in that split second. I connect what I see to an emotion I feel inside.

If an image is even slightly 'out', I won't print it. It may look right to others but, for me, the skill is in the taking.

After I've taken a photograph, I leave it be until I feel the need to look at it again. Really look at it. Understand its nuances. Feel where it wants some darkness lifted, some extra light allowed in, some emphasis in a particular area. I never alter the image. I work with it. I listen to what it wants to say. I work on an image only once I feel I have become the subject. I ask myself what metaphor, what emotion the subject is portraying.

I never ask with my mind and the chaos and confusion that is inherently packaged with the mind. I always pay attention from no-mind, that place of under-water awareness and connectivity to my innocent child-like self. In order to do that, I have to wait until I am in a no-mind state. I can't just sit down on a random morning after breakfast and get busy.

The Jetty

In working with the images, I am actually working with myself. Each image mirrors back to me an emotion I may have been dealing with when I took the shot – or an emotion I am dealing with as I work with it.

Each image enables me to question myself. Where in my life am I like this? Or, perhaps, where in my life do I need this?

Years after taking *The Boat* image, it allows me to connect with that serene part inside myself and that is also in each and every one of us. If we don't feel serene it's because we have not looked in the right place within us. Looking at it is like spending an hour in a monastery. It removes my anxiety. It grounds me. It reminds me that deep within me stillness resides. Without that stillness I could not have seen or experienced this image. My images create emotional, spiritual healing, even in me. They are my way of communicating with myself. Sometimes, like with this image I could burst into tears when I stare at it. I can feel the presence of God staring back at me.

All of us have such opportunities. Not necessarily in what we do, but in the way that we do it. As I now understand it, the way we do things needs to be responsive rather than reactive.

What's the difference?

Well, so many of our actions are moulded by incidents from our childhood years. What we think now is simply a repetition or knock-on effect of those events. It's a knee-jerk, automatic reaction that kicks in when a circumstance that seems similar confronts us.

Zebras

The knee-jerk reaction is one of the reasons I believe that every person should do some sort of therapy – or that it should be compulsory at school. We desperately need some insight into the workings of our emotions. We need to be aware that the emotion we are constantly suppressing and not giving expression to will end up making us feel depressed and drive us unwittingly into, for instance, one relationship after another, thinking we'll find ourselves in another person.

In contrast to a reaction, a response has a pause in it. We listen. We understand. Then we respond - relevantly.

Life holds up a mirror for us, inviting us to face our early conditioning and to reconsider that conditioning in the light of what we have learned about ourselves. We can react – and remain stuck. Or we can respond – and grow.

In that context, it's important to remember that we are all one another in a different form. I have the same emotions as you do. Anger, fear, love... If I've got what you've got, just in another form, then at our deepest cores, as spirit, we are not separate. Water remains water, whether it's in a jug, falling as rain, coloured, still, or sparkling, or a single droplet of water in the ocean.

So, we are mirrors, one of another. When we are yelling at someone behind a counter, we're actually yelling at some part of ourselves that we have refused to own. When we start to dig around in our emotional closets, we will see that we actually have the trait we don't like in someone else. When we understand the concept of 'I am you, in another form,' that we have everything that we see in others, our lives are altered forever, because we expand and grow continuously.

We've spent our lives believing what we were taught: that we are different from everyone else. We see ourselves in competition with the world, me against you.

One of the great eye-openers for me was realising that I have everything I love in me, and that everything I hate about others is also in me. I've even been guilty of murder, in terms of squashing someone else's idea or enthusiasm.

Once we are open to owning every single trait in the universe, we can stop pretending that we are better than other people. The key is perceiving that there is nothing that we are not.

I spent a lot of time projecting my shortcomings on to others. I stopped when I saw that when I was judging others I was, in fact, judging myself. Our shadows are often hidden so well that we ourselves cannot find them. I've watched intellectually powerful people, including close friends and family, struggle to identify their own faults using their own intellect. They understand the concept but cannot relate it to themselves.

When you do find a way to do that, a small portal in your psyche opens and light streams in to it. You can live your life blinded by the things that others see in you so clearly. You can be infatuated with something or someone, which blinds you to everything else. You see only the positives. To me it's as though you are disowning parts of yourself and projecting them on to someone else.

What does 'projecting our feelings on to others' mean? I knew the phrase but had never witnessed myself projecting myself on to others until I matured enough to get a bird's eye view of my actions. I saw just how much my childhood patterns were affecting my relationships and my life. If I had loneliness in me, I was thinking that no matter what relationship I went into, I would be lonely and my partner would be the cause of that.

Having been an empath all my life, I still struggle with co-dependency, feeling that I need others to help me succeed. I believe there is such a high divorce rate because it's easier for people to blame the other person rather than to take responsibility for their own emotions. "You make me feel like this..." Until you do take responsibility for the way you are feeling, nothing is going to change.

Learning to master your own emotions should be a school subject or, at the very least, an extra-mural activity. How else can children, whether they've been traumatized or not, learn to cope?

Why have we all gone quietly along with whomever made that first decision that emotions are bad things and should, therefore, be excluded from formal schooling and life in general? Why do we agree to an education system that deliberately does not nurture children's emotions, their spirits?

Why do we admire a way of life that forces us to be competitive, removed from others and ourselves, and to play the game. Why do we not hold peaceful, simple people in high regard?

There are no guarantees that wisdom and insight and connection to Self will develop automatically as we mature. The majority of people in their 60s, 70s, and 80s are tired, grumpy, and miserable because they have allowed the box-in system to rule their lives. I've met some younger people who are rebelling against being boxed in and who say they want change and don't want to end up emotionally crippled like their parents. But most of them don't have the grounding in nature and God. They're trapped in a world of technology, drifting steadily into becoming removed from themselves.

No one has taught us how to be human. In turn, we're not instilling into the next generation what we've learned. Are we just too afraid of doing the emotional work?

Because of that fear, it's important to respond compassionately to the images our mirrors are holding up to us. They're there to help us understand ourselves so that we can evolve and, eventually, move closer to our essence, our soul.

As mirrors to ourselves, we learn that we owe ourselves compassion. As mirrors to others, we learn that love and kindness are the only emotions that will enable us to grow. Anything else will hold us back. And, as others mirror us, gratitude to them and to the lessons they offer us is the only response that empowers us.

It's hard work. It means realising that everyone and everything you look at is a mirror. It means looking in the mirror 24 hours a day.

It feels much easier to stay closed, shut off, and defensive. Actually, it takes far less energy to pro-actively ride the mirror roller-coaster and become your core, true self than to cling desperately to the superficial you, who is simply a collection of ideas, concepts, and opinions and, therefore, isn't real.

Once you ask for change, your soul is on a mission. Then it has the power of a river in flood. It will sweep you along.

Your soul is waiting for you to ask for change. Allow yourself to be swept along.

Owning our shadows

Because I have come to know that everything in life is a mirror in which I can see aspects of myself that need attention or care or love, I was intrigued to find myself having taken this picture of a sunset in South Africa's remote, rural area called the Transkei.

Like a few of my other images at the time (and the one in the previous chapter), this one included a boat. But, overall, it was very different from all of the rest. In fact, it was different from 45 years of images. Because the sun was setting everything was in silhouette. It emphasised the long shadows laid down by the setting sun, rather than the light reflected in the river and the clouds.

My spiritual teacher told me that boats are symbols for travelling into the subconscious mind, the Self.

In this particular case, my soul must have been on its own mission. At the time of taking the photograph, I was doing some deep inner work, going back to my childhood memories and experiences, including my Dad's death. I was not conscious of what the boat represented. I was just drawn to it.

In some way, therefore, I may have taken this photograph in my childhood. It had travelled with me, subconsciously, for all these years until, one day, at the right time in my spiritual evolution, I came across an external representation of what I needed to deal with internally. My subconscious used the physical boat to call my attention to my spiritual work.

When I first thought about things from this unusual perspective, I felt that I might be a little crazy. Then I discovered that other people have the same kinds of experiences. In any case, I've

River Boat

known for many years that very often the subconscious communicates with us through images. They're all around us. We simply don't realise they're tools for us to use, so we look past them or ignore them. I couldn't ignore this nudge from my subconscious. My work, as you can see from the images on preceding pages, is usually very light.

Initially, I wanted to push the picture away. I was reluctant to work on it. I didn't want to show it to people. Part of me felt that, because the image was so different, it would scare people. It would not lift them as my other photos do.

Then I realised that my resistance actually came from my not wanting to show the world that there is also a dark side to me. I get angry. I get depressed. I've always suffered from anxiety. I have my own struggles with 'the dark night of the soul'. Just because I have been given an ability to capture the beauty of the essence of light does not mean that I have no emotional pain; that I am not flawed as a person.

I realised that refusing to show and share that side of me made me one-dimensional. Incomplete. How could I teach essence in my workshops without acknowledging the role of darkness in bringing about healing?

This image has forced me to work with the darkness in myself. It has taken me months to work with the picture, carefully looking for the photographic information that is always present in the dark areas of an image. As one lightens the picture, so detail begins to emerge.

Desert Tree

Exactly the same thing happens as I work with myself while I'm working with the image. I shine a small, gentle light into my shadow self and it offers me information about my fears and anxieties and how to heal them. The more of myself I reveal, the more I heal. Healing is about becoming whole. Ignoring my shadow information leaves me incomplete, not whole. Working with my shadow information brings me closer to embracing my whole self.

The Boat image is symbolic on other levels, too. The rocks represent the hard, rigid parts of me that I've bashed myself against or have learned to steer around. Interesting that the rocks are mostly piled up on one side...

The water, of course, symbolises emotions. The boat allows one to float over or on top of one's emotions rather than swimming in them, getting to grips with them.

The Boat image is a journey into yourself. I have had to go gently, quietly, uncovering the image, feeling with it – and with my shadow. I can face only so many fears at any given time. I can handle only so much change, which triggers my fear, at a time. Everything is designed to open space up inside of us.

 Because I am the same as you, *The Boat* image is also an invitation for you: 'Let's go through the dark together. Let's see what it contains. There's information for us.'

Everyone's darkness is painful. It's a place where we usually choose not to go. It contains memories and emotions from our childhood that become the reasons for our attracting certain types of negativity into our adult lives. When I was growing up there was never enough. I felt I had to work harder so I would not end up like my family. There was a sense that there wasn't enough to go around – not enough money, not enough time, not enough love. This can be described by the term poverty consciousness which impacts all of us in all parts of our lives where we often feel we don't even deserve love or to be loved.

As I said earlier, I believe everyone needs some kind of therapy. Not necessarily in the formal form of a therapist who asks us how we feel, but someone who is able to sit beside us and hold the space for us. Perhaps not say much, but simply listen and reflect (like a mirror) some important things back to us, so that we can solve our own problems.

Instead, we struggle on alone, repressing feelings and memories until, in our forties and fifties, the negativity begins to express itself in our bodies as aches and pains or illness.

Obedient to the system that has groomed us, we never question what has happened to us. We still colour inside the lines. We stay controlled by conventional thinking. We focus on goals and achievements, thinking they will make us happy.

My sister's unexpected death showed me just how divorced and disconnected our external personalities are from our souls. She did not realise she was dying. When I wanted to take her to the emergency room, she told me I was over-reacting. She was gone a few hours later.

In one way, I take her over-reaction statement as a message to me that she wasn't going to 'end'. She would continue, somewhere. It's just that I would not be able to see and talk to her on this plane.

Just as importantly, though, her death also showed me that I didn't understand the word 'die'. We think that death marks the end of our life. In fact, we are dying each-and-every day. In the obvious sense, we're ageing, getting closer to death. In a more subtle sense, we're moving on from old habits, from relationships and belief systems which are no longer beneficial to us. The external world changes. Seasons, politicians, economics move through cycles. All this change is a good thing. We're advancing in understanding. But it invariably feels painful.

For example, for me, turning 50 was painful. I did not understand the new person I had to become. My body was changing, my surroundings were shifting. There were things I could not hold on to any longer. Of course, I could (should?) have looked at it as an adventure. Instead, I found it trying. I had to work on taking the Alice in Wonderland approach and stop wanting things to stay the same.

I now know that death, in terms of the soul departing from the body, means leaving behind everything material. That includes your physical body and the personality you acquire as part of the process of living a material life. But, your essence continues.

Which means that the essence, your soul, is the reality. It's what really matters. The material world is temporary, mostly painful, and simply a dance with life. It's not Life itself.

The interesting thing, though, is that to access Life itself, you need to dance with full awareness. You need to be awake as you dance. I've learned that when I'm awake, in flow, that's when my best work is done. I'm actually dancing with my soul, fully connected to who I am.

When I'm in flow, I do believe I become a walking subconscious mind. Often, in that state at night, I will have a dream that is quite radical or extreme. Invariably the dream is my subconscious mind trying to bring some information into my conscious mind.

For me, the 'dark' image of *The Boat* is Jungian, an archetype, in the same way that my dreams are. The boat is able to take me to the places in myself to which I'd rather not go.

It often feels as if it would be easier to go and live in a monastery or a cave, to avoid the harshness of the material life. But, as I see things now, we have to be monks living a normal life. We have to be in flow in spite of all the distractions.

I agree with Caroline Myss's challenge to conventional thinking about purpose when she asks the question: "What if your life's purpose is simply to shine the light in your neighbourhood?" That seems terribly simplistic and possibly even boring. Yet, as she points out, we are where we are, doing what we do, for a reason. We may not understand the reason. All we need to know is that we have been given certain tasks in this life and the way we do them is what matters.

Even if we're not South African, all of us know what it's like to be stuck on a wag-'n-bietjie bush. It's an indigenous South African bush with curved thorns. Once you're caught, it's very difficult to unhook yourself. It symbolises our insistence on wanting to go in one direction, getting hooked on to the physical world, while life pushes us in another direction – towards essence. As John Lennon put it: 'Life is what happens when you are busy making other plans.'

Of course, we struggle. And the more we struggle, the more caught-up we get.

The *River Boat* image showed me that, although I don't want darkness and struggle, I do need to own my darkness, my struggle. I have to own all the fragments of myself. Otherwise, there is no way I can be whole. Wholeness is vital because it's the only way to calm down the emotional chaos in ourselves – and to 'shine the light in our neighbourhood.'

Suffering is optional

Shielded by a comfortable upbringing and a materially successful career, it took me decades to realise how much suffering there is in this life. I got my first inklings of this truth when I started the Buckaroo Project, which raises funds and arranges for the sterilisation of dogs living in South Africa's poverty-stricken townships.

The number of dogs in the townships explodes exponentially because their owners cannot afford the high vet bills for sterilisation. At the same time, there just isn't enough food to feed the human families, let alone their animal hangers-on.

The cycle of suffering just keeps rolling. What makes it worse is that people who could afford the time and the money to help simply turn a blind eye. This has changed both my view on life and my life considerably. Very often, the very thing we're afraid of becomes the lesson we have to learn.

There are some people who are terrified of going into the townships where people's poverty is all too obvious and the dogs are often terribly thin. I, too, was one of those. So, doing the work with the dogs became a huge lesson for me in facing my own emotional poverty, pain, and starvation. It made me come face-to-face with myself, only to be greeted by a wagging tail and a lick of gratitude from the dogs. I believe the dogs balance the sometimes negative energy in poverty-stricken areas. In spite of living in such harsh conditions, they always wag their tails. They remind me of the statues of the Buddha – mostly smiling. There has to be a subconscious reason why the word 'dog' spelt backwards is symbolic of all we are meant to be. Being forced by my compassion for the dogs to face my own pain, I realised that I will never betray my own soul.

Lion Cubs

As I begged and borrowed resources from friends, family, and professional people to build the project, I gradually realised that I was rebuilding my own crumbling emotional foundations. The obstacles I encountered with the people involved in the project were the early steps in my unravelling my own shadow self.

There was a point when no food was coming into the project. So, I went and stood outside a local retail store, asking shoppers as they went in to donate a tin or bag of food as they came out. I ended up collecting 10 trolley loads of food. But, I felt like a beggar. I'm reasonably well-known in town, both because of my images and my teaching at the local college and now with my regular private workshops.

People commented and some even sneered. My ego took quite a hammering. If I could have, I'd have had other people stand there instead of me. No-one else was willing to do it. But I clung to: 'Ask and ye shall receive.' The secret one is not told about asking is that, in order to receive, you have to actually show up. You have to stand at the door of the store.

I found myself asking God: "Why are you making me do this?"

The very clear answer I got was: "This is just a test of your endurance. You say you love the dogs and you want to make a difference in this world. Are you willing to hand over your ego?"

Well, I was not willing to face the dogs with no food. Obviously, my ego had to go.

It was fascinating, though, to watch people walk a little faster to

Umntwana (A Child in Xhosa language)

get into the shop before I could intercept them. By and large, people don't want to get involved. Perhaps they don't have the extra cash. Perhaps their own lives are too difficult to have capacity for others' pain.

I've done the same.

The dogs changed me. Not long after my begging experience, I came across a down-and-out person outside a different shop trying to sell for R10 some elastic bracelets she had made.

Instead of walking on by, trying not to meet her eyes and possibly even being irritable, I gave her R20. I thought of telling her to keep the bracelet, so that she could sell it to someone else. But that would have been insulting. She was offering an item of value. I took it with thanks and, some time later, I gave it to a petrol attendant who really wanted it.

Interesting, isn't it, how life is full of chain reactions. One experience influences how one behaves in the next one. I try, now, to be aware of the consequences of my actions.

There is a flip side to helping, though. I have a strong tendency, when I see suffering, to want to fix people and circumstances. On one of Buckaroo's volunteer trips into the townships, a young man in his twenties offered his help with the dogs. Over time, he became my translator for the Xhosa people who owned the dogs. Xhosa is the language spoken in the area where I live.

Thinking I could give him a hand up, I took him out of his situation to work as a gardener in the sacred space around my Centre of

Africanis

Light and Photography. Little did I know that he was a drugs and alcohol addict.

He was able to keep his addictions under control for three months but then the need for his fix became greater than the need to grow and improve himself. He was filled with remorse, and I was left with a hollow heart. The situation caused us to part ways. It is amazing how certain people come into your life as triggers that unleash emotional pain. This youngster helped me to get in touch with issues around my father onto which I was holding.

But, the situation taught me that it's not possible to fix people. They must walk their own road, and dance to their own tune. They must also want to be helped.

Reviewing what had happened, I saw very clearly that some people come into your life just for a season, while others may be with you for a life-time.

Perhaps, though, the unmistakable lesson is that suffering of whatever kind is a question: Are you prepared to help? More importantly, are you prepared to hand over your ego in order to help?

When I see people who are strolling on the beach ignore a piece of plastic and not bend to pick it up or walk past thin dogs and starving people, I recognise myself before the Buckaroo project. I was one of those people who would not go to the SPCA or a dog shelter because I knew it would upset me. I knew help was needed, but couldn't bring myself to do anything. So, I was of no use to the dogs.

It wasn't until something drove me to go into the townships and I was ripped open emotionally by the suffering I saw there that I actually began to be of use to those in need. I began to make a difference. It only takes one person to start the process of helping.

When I've spent a day in the townships, I cry myself to sleep. I wake up worrying about a dog or an owner. But, at least I feel I am being what a human should be. I may be emotionally shredded but I'm not as hurt and lost and lonely and vulnerable as the dogs tied up with barbed wire and left without food and water in the heat of an African day.

We will all experience pain in our lives, but we don't have to suffer if we choose to look at the cause of the pain. The question for all of us has to be, then: 'Where do I begin and when do I decide that I can make a difference?'

Unconditional Love

Although I made sure I did well at school – because, like everyone else, I wanted to fit in – I struggled mightily to master formal analytical disciplines like maths and the rigid grammar of language. The intuitive aspects of education, like the rhythm and musical aspects of language, came more readily.

As a result, I became acutely aware of the full spectrum of communication - all the way from the tone and colouration of spoken words, to the subtler layers of communication, including: body language, breathing, and the energy expressed through the eyes.

This made me able to communicate with animals. I could understand them, because I sensed their energy state. Like me, they're not interested in mental anlaysis. They don't judge you by what you're wearing, what car you drive, or where you live. They care only about your energy state.

They don't want to know what you're thinking. They want to know who you really are, inside yourself.

And they respond accordingly.

Because they operate naturally from no-mind, they operate instinctively from a basis of love. We tend to use the word love very loosely. My work with nature and her animals has shown me that we don't really understand the word at all. A mother, for instance, will say she loves her child. Sometimes, what she thinks is love is actually a form of neediness and clinging.

I saw that first with the dogs who were my best childhood friends. In later years, the township dogs with whom my Buckaroo Project

Misty Morning

interacts proved to me again that animals' inherent bias is towards love. The Buckaroo dogs are invariably starving or, at least, extremely hungry. And, yes, they will come gladly to us for the food they know we have. Always, though, they will show appreciation - wagging their tails, licking our hands, standing up on their hind legs to greet us -before eating anything. They want love more than they want food and they return every morsel of love they receive from us.

Their love is unconditional. It's not dependent on whether we feed them or not. It's entirely in response to our attitudes to them. They remain loyal and kind towards owners who may starve, hit, or chain them – or leave them outside in all weathers.

Humans call themselves higher beings. In fact, it's animals who are effortlessly spiritually and emotionally noble. They are able to forget their own pain in order to sense yours and comfort you.

On one trip into a township that we'd been visiting for about 10 months, events in my personal life had left me feeling depressed.

An old dog, who was quite aggressive and whose owners wanted him euthenised because they saw him as a nuisance, came up to me, put his head on my chest and pushed into me a little. Previously, I had not been able to touch him or even look him directly in the eye. He'd been aware of our kindness through the months and now he figured it was time for him to repay it. He was prepared to let go of his anger because my need was greater than his.

We all live according to our own value systems, of course. My particular system is a negation of everything the material world holds dear and focuses instead on spirituality as expressed through nature in general and animals in particular. At times, I've congratulated myself on having what seems to me to be a relatively pure value system.

It came as something of a shock, therefore, to realise that neither the animals I so love nor nature herself have - or need - a value system. Everything that happens with them is about the present moment. If there's food, I eat. If my children need protecting, I spring to their defense. If there's a human whose energy levels are depleted, I put my head on her chest.

Birds just live. They wake up, they look for food, they feed their chicks, they roost when the sun goes down. They don't plan or scheme or worry. Sure, their needs are basic. But, then, actually, so are ours.

It's tempting to think that animals don't plan or scheme or worry because they can't. Not so. If you really look into an animal's eyes, you will see there is someone there. Aware. Awake. Interested. Loving.

They speak. We just don't know how to hear them. They call us to question our mad race for achievements, our incessant accumulation of stuff, our desperate hunt for relationships, our clinging to mental concepts.

They call us to remember that, when we die, we can take none of that with us.

They remind us that nature should be our guide, our guru.

Everything natural knows when to be born, when to flower, when to bear fruit, when to simply let go and return to Source.

The message couldn't be clearer. Let go of your belief systems. They only exist above your shoulders, in your mind which, in itself, doesn't exist. The mind is still a mystery to this day. Yet, we allow it to dominate and rule our lives.

The belief systems that the mind creates limit you. These systems restrict you to what the mind knows. And, as I've said, the mind only knows what it has learned from other people and their limited belief systems. It knows nothing about the 'truth,' which is accessible only through that place of child-like innocence, no-mind.

Lily Pond

Once you're awake, you can't go back to sleep

I don't profess to have all the answers to the big questions of Life. What I'm offering here is the substance of years of questioning the conventional answers we are given by what, for lack of a simpler phrase, I call the system.

Some of the insights I've stumbled on may be of use to you as you do your own dance with Life. All of us looking for the real answers to the big questions have something to offer all of the others.

In effect, we are hypnotised from birth by our culture, our parents, and our teachers. We learn about life from these powerful influencers. We need to wake up from this state, which the Eastern philosophies, including Buddhism and Hinduism, call Maya. It's a state of illusion. It distorts our perception of the world. And, it's not a normal state. Being aware, awake, and living from spirit is our natural state. But, until we question the conventions we are taught, we cannot reclaim and live in that natural state.

We have to ask ourselves why we continue to do the same crazy stuff over-and- over and why we don't make changes even though we know what we are doing is not beneficial to us.

Due to our fear of the unknown (all the things, including emotions, that are at our core but are not visible to our external eyes), we distract ourselves with all sorts of things. We seek artificial connections almost all of the time because we spend most of our time in our heads. We seriously believe that, if we just get that one thing or one person, our lives will be better. We then spend our whole lives tricking ourselves into believing we are connected to that one thing or person. Sadly, the more we do this the further we drift away from our true essence.

Sky View

We don't know who we really are underneath all of our distractions. We believe what we do is who we are. We are not that. We get lost in the outside world because we are not taught from childhood to watch our thinking.

I was lucky. Instinctively, but without realising exactly what I was doing, I began dancing with my emotions. Without a spiritual rudder, though, I often felt I was drowning. It was only in adult-hood, when the pain became too great, that I realised I wasn't supposed to be drowning. I told myself I didn't want to feel that way anymore. I didn't want my life to be run by my anxiety and my reactive nature.

Thank goodness for that pain threshold – the realisation that I could not do that anymore! It's what forces us to make the changes we've been avoiding. The turning point for me was noticing that I had an equal amount of bad stuff in me as I had good. Simulta-neously, I began to understand what was my stuff and what was someone else's.

For many years, I was close to someone who over-reacted to the smallest problem. I then reacted and we'd end up in a serious argument. Now, I am able to observe myself and stay in my body and distinguish between my issues and theirs. We have virtually no arguments, now, because I chose not to be a part of their issues. I chose to shed light on my shadow.

It needs only one person in the relationship to do this. An argument cannot exist without two people. The challenge is to step back in order to observe yourself in the heat of the moment. That's usually when you are swept away by your ego and emotions.
The more you're able to observe your reactions, the more light you will shed on this part of your shadow and, gradually, it will lift and the dynamics of the relationship will change.

All of what I've observed about myself as I've danced with Life is expressed in my images in various ways.

As you will have seen throughout this book, no single image is a complete expression of who I am. It's an expression of the space

Sun Dance

I was in and the understanding I had at the time I took the photograph. That's because the dance with Life goes on - every day, every minute, I dance. Sometimes I am leading, sometimes I'm following. Sometimes I'm gliding smoothly across the floor and the lights and music are just right. Sometimes I feel as if I have two left feet, I can't pick up the rhythm, and the music is just plain annoying. It's important to put a healthy structure in place to keep us on track, to keep us aligned. Where we put our focus is what takes over our emotions.

We have to learn to become our own coach, to help navigate ourselves back to truth. It is important to prepare ourselves throughout the day to be human. My understanding at the moment is that however the dance is going today, you need to take enjoyment in the difference you make. Because, ultimately, you're making a difference for your own sake. Of course it's helpful to others but, in essence, doing good feels good to you.

It gives meaning to one's own existence. Also, after all the years of dancing, I'm fully awake in two particularly profound ways. Firstly, I know in every fibre of my being that I am not going to be here forever. Secondly, I am also very aware that once you are awake to yourself you can never go back to sleep again. Most of us know this fact intellectually. But do we really know what it means? Do we live each day in the absolute knowledge that we are simply passing through this place, this space, this time?

We humans don't belong here, on this planet. Countless times I've watched animals run from humans. But, I've never seen a dog, for instance, run from a tree, or the waves of the sea, or the moonlight. It's not just that we don't fit here. We're scary. We're aliens, because we've forgotten who we really are.

It's as though we were given a candy store but didn't read the rules about eating only one chocolate a week in order to achieve true freedom. If you sit and savour it, you can own the whole chain of candy stores throughout the country. Instead, we shovel candy into our mouths – grabbing, running and getting super sick on a sugar high.

Mind-driven as we choose to be, we almost refuse to connect with the essence, spirit, energy that is the Source of the planet and everything it contains. System-bound as we are taught to be, we get worked up over stuff that is ultimately irrelevant. We flutter and bash ourselves against the bars of the material cage we insisted on getting into ourselves.

All of us know someone who has spent his/her life accumulating wealth but has no health. He/She has made him/herself sick in the fight to accumulate the wealth. Now he/she must use his/her money to buy the medical advice and medicines and supplements that will help him/her slow her life down. Isn't it bizarre that it costs money to be healthy in a life focused on money?

Many-a-time, I've sat on my verandah, watching a wild dove sun itself. Its wings are stretched to catch the full benefit of the warmth. Its head is held up to the sun, eyes closed in bliss. It gives itself completely to the moment.

And then, a human being living a box existence (with a box-house, box-car, box-office, box-bedroom), shoots the dove for making a mess on their house box. Now there's a value system of which to be proud!

We think we are our boxes, our families, our education, our country. What if we're not? How can we be, if none of it is going with us one day?

In chatting to a group of primary school children being given a tour around my Centre of Light and Photography, I asked how many of them experienced anxiety. Half of them put up their hands. I was intrigued by the fact that such young children understood what anxiety is and how many were suffering from it. They're at a stage of their lives where they're discovering all sorts of new things. That should be an adventure, not a reason to be anxious.

I gave a presentation about Buckaroo to a school in a reasonably poor area of town. All the children in the school had been brought into the hall, with the youngest seated on my left and the high school children on my right. The teachers were dotted around on chairs against the walls.

The difference in energy from the three different audiences in that one hall was remarkable. You can see when the spirit is home. There's a light in the eyes, a smile on the lips, a freedom of engagement with the world. The younger children were all awake and present. The older children were dull and heavy-spirited, lacking in interest and volition. The teachers were slumped and tired.

There, in front of me, was the system in a nutshell. The system discourages individuality. You must conform. Wear your uniform. Hurry up. Stand in line to get on the conveyor belt so that you can regurgitate what someone else has thought and then be spewed out, thoroughly bleached of yourself, into the world of work – often to become a teacher for the next generation of aliens on Earth.

In the field

If only someone had given me a map

Part of the reason I emphasise the system, is that I now realise my life has been a journey against the system. Not overtly and, until recently, not consciously. I am not confrontational by nature. I hate ugliness and physical, mental, and emotional violence. It is impossible for me to produce my photographs in a confrontational or violent state of mind.

To be who I am and, thereby, to make the difference that I am able to by producing images that touch people deeply enough for them to make life changes, I have to be the opposite of the system. I have to be awake, aware, conscious of essence. Deeply and profoundly still.

It would have been great if a teacher in first grade had given me a map to Life. It would have saved me a lot of time on my journey to myself. I could have been still and awake decades ago.

On the other hand, having to discover that there actually is a system and then having to find my own path out of it gives me the right to say there is another way.

My images, my video series, "*Capturing What People Don't Talk About,*" my first book, *Sky meets Land*, and my courses are proof of another way.

There was a time when I would run from my negative emotions. Then I discovered they followed me.

Now, I sit with them. As the Buddhists teach, when you simply watch your thoughts and emotions arise, they leave as quickly as they come. It's only when we dwell on them, cling to them, rehash them over and over again, that they refuse to leave.

Animals are instinctive Buddhists. They'll show a flash of anger or sorrow and, within minutes, they'll be their usual selves. After years of appalling abuse, they will still offer love.

So, it seems to me as though we have to die to our emotions, by surrendering not to the emotion itself but to its presence in our minds and bodies. We will not live forever and we don't know how much time we have left. Why let any of that time be overwhelmed by negativity when letting go and allowing things to be are available to us?

When I started writing this book, I had embarked on a return to my photographic roots in black-and-white images. I could feel that my inner journey had brought me to a point where clarity and purity were my objectives and I wanted to show others how to find their own purity and clarity. Essence and spirit are most easily visible when the clutter of colour is stripped away.

During the time of writing this book, I underwent many experiences – such as the death of my sister – that were entirely new to me. I struggled with the emotions they stirred in me. I felt that the emotional tools I had put together so painstakingly over 50 years were insufficient. That the dark times were bigger than I was.

And then came *The Boat* image. It was an emotional pivot. It showed me that I had both the strength and the wisdom to move on to a richer, more empowered phase of my life. The image wasn't the mechanism that shifted me. It was the evidence that I had already shifted. Awakening brings more responsibility. You have to say goodbye to your old identity and become ready to embody a new version of yourself.

That is not the end, however. The dance with life stops only when we take our last breath – and perhaps not even then. Science tells us that energy cannot ever be destroyed. It simply changes from one form to another. For me, Life is energy. Everything is energy. With this knowledge underpinning everything I do now, a new phase is opening up for me.

I've begun to take very different photographs...

Forest Dance

Forest Walk

'I can't see the forest for the trees,' is such an accurate reflection of the way most of us live. We spend so much of our lives on focusing on details that we seldom sit back and see the big picture.

So, it comes as a surprise to find that the answers to the questions: 'What is this life?', and 'Why are we here?' do actually exist. We've just been unable or unwilling to hear them.

My mother was an exception to that rule. In her 80s, she retained a powerful faith in God and all the vital spiritual things that we cannot see with our external eyes. She always told me her faith would get her through anything.

I thought I had things figured out, too. I was quite in tune with life and nature and, so I believed, had a pretty good understanding of how everything worked.

The death of my sister, Jenny, lifted that veil away from me.

At first, the grief was heavy and dense. It was all the harder to bear each time Mom cried. Gradually, though, I surfaced into the insight that we're all going to die. That liberated me. I saw so clearly how absurd it is that we take so much for granted and how unnecessary our worry is.

If we know that we're going to die one day, then what is the point of killing one another – or fighting every day for survival?

As Eckhart Tolle says, 'We are unconscious. If we were conscious, we would be celebrating life, knowing that none of the stuff we bother so much about matters as much as we get trapped into

Vine Leaf

thinking it does. We would make our spirituality our highest value and keep that as a focus, a priority.'

In my view, life is the breath. We can have possessions and relationships but, without breath we do not have life. Real life is also about being alone. It's a way of flying without wings. It's a way of seeing past the confusion of the trees to the glorious wholeness of the entire forest.

For three days at the Buddhist retreat centre, I danced through the forest going deeper and deeper into the woods. In fact, the forest was overwhelming. Like life, there was just so much to look at and absorb. The only way I could cope was by taking my camera each morning and looking at the tiniest leaves I could find. I related to the forest as being a microcosm of the universe.

Always, we have universes within universes right in front of us. Any small piece of overgrown property has so much going on in the undergrowth and all of it is linked directly to God.

I hadn't taken a tripod on the trip. I panicked a bit, because the camera was heavy. But the early morning light dancing through the trees enchanted and mesmerised me. Everything was so still, I could hear the whispering of the nature spirits. I never felt alone. In fact, I know for sure I was not alone.

I rarely do much macro work but, on those mornings at the retreat, it was macro work that wanted to be done. I just could not get enough. The shapes, the sounds, the smells of the forest, the moist feeling of the moss on the bark became an extraordinary spiritual experience. I became the forest.

Although everything was overwhelmingly beautiful, I focused on the light on the tiniest of leaves.

Like the *River Boat* image was an entirely new type of photograph for me, the images in my Forest Range are yet again completely different to anything I have photographed before. I believe they represent a new beginning for me, both photographically and in terms of my spiritual evolution.

The forest trip was a bit like falling down one of <u>Alice in Wonderland's</u> rabbit holes. I had no idea where I was going or what the next stage of my life would bring. And that was completely and wonderfully OK.

We humans have become disastrously removed from the truth and so very few of us follow the path to the inner world. I love the term 'inner engineer.' I like being an inner engineer - reconstructing myself continuously through my images.

And so I want to say: have gratitude for your life, the abundance of it, and the fact that it will not last forever. Feel that as deeply in your fibre as you can.

If you're feeling down and empty, it will be because of your pattern of thinking about things. It's an artificial pattern overlayed on you by the system. You can change it any time you want to do so.

Find a positive video or workshop to help you reprogramme your thinking – You could start with my YouTube channel. Know that we are doing what we're meant to be doing in the place we're meant to be. If the doing and the place feel negative, change your thinking about them.

Start dancing. Dance in your heart. Life is one big, long dance. The music doesn't end. There is no one final moment. Everything is always happening all of the time. There is no end to which to get. Just keep moving and flowing with the rhythm of life.

I've had some humdingers of depression, feeling as if I am suffocating. But I know now I cannot blame the situation, my country, my neighbours, my partners. Sometimes it is necessary to leave a situation. Not because you are running away, but because you are strong enough to stand in your own light, to live your purpose unaffected by other people's opinions and needs.

You leave because you have found YOU again. You have managed to tap into the essence that is inside of you. The spirit that is you. The rhythm that makes your heart sing.

If you run, you will simply attract more of the things from which you are running. And, yes, sometimes you have to run in order to give yourself the time and space to find yourself. But run, then, towards the song that is inside of you.

We are all pushing against something. The energy we use to cover up our magic is exhausting, draining. Focus on what lifts your spirit. Spend moments with yourself - just have an ice-cream because it makes you feel good. Do something that nurtures you.

My feel-good place is nature. I love listening to the birds, animals. The sea is my favourite spot. A swim in the ocean cleanses my aura, raises my vibration, and makes me feel like I am flying. It centres me!

Do the things of which you have dreamed. Most importantly, love

Zen Leaves

yourself. You are truly all you have and the lessons you have been given, no matter how tough, are there precisely to toughen you up – not to make you roll over and give up.

A few years ago I walked on hot coals. Apparently, they were hotter than most. What carried me over them without getting burned was the determination in me that those coals would not burn me. I crossed them three times in a row to prove to myself that I really could decide not to be burned – and not burn. We can all do it.

It's a state of being. It's the state of being that enables me to swim most mornings in the icy-cold ocean. Just knowing we are not here forever makes me say to my Maker: 'Here I am. I am here to meet you and embrace everything that you have given me, everything I am.'

Until we rise up and meet our shadow selves and learn to love that part of us as well as acknowledging that we have everything inside of us, including our enemies, we cannot master ourselves. Embrace everything, dance with it all late at night and in the early hours of the morning. Wrestle with it, fall over with it, but don't blame anyone, especially not yourself. Blame weakens you. Embracing every part of you is the way to win the battle against depression, anxiety, and loneliness. It's the way to win back your life so that you can continue to dance.

Forest Walk I

Light and Dark dance together

As an ocean person, I used to think of the forest as a dark place. As a light-chaser in more ways than one, I like happy, light things. So, when I looked at the body of work that came out of my time on the mountain at the Buddhist retreat centre, I thought I must have been depressed when I took the images. They were dark and focused in on tiny detail.

Actually, the images are the result of my reflecting on and integrating a whole new aspect of myself: where the light meets the dark.

I had just been through a year of working on my shadow - looking at why I didn't stand up for myself, why I allowed people to emotionally abuse me, why I allowed myself to be manipulated so. I looked at so many things for so long that it felt as if I was dying.

Going up the mountain and into the forest felt like it was my last hope to reconnect with myself. As I started to find the tiniest fern growing out of an embankment - and another and then another, it wasn't long before I began to see an immense amount of light coming in through the trees and shining on these little beings. The leaves became my friends, as did the frogs and the moss growing on the trees. There were moments when I felt an extreme tingling sensation of aliveness wash through me. There was so much life there. I zoomed in to hug tree ferns about to unfold their tiny arms to the light. In fact, everything was stretching and beaming towards the light. I was so excited that I began to beam the light within myself. It was as though I had had fairy forest dust sprinkled all over me. Who would have thought that so much intensity could be so light?

Then came the moment I had felt for which I had lived my entire

Forest Walk II

life. At the bottom of the path down deep into the forest, I saw a dam. Still, quiet, dark rich brown in colour, because of all the pine needles lying thick at the bottom.

I was aware that it's very good to be around pine trees because they absorb and cure emotional pain in humans and the environment. I knew I was in good company.

I sat quietly on a small wooden jetty that was probably as old as the retreat centre. Even though there was a high likelihood of their being snakes around, I removed my boots and socks and gently laid my camera on the ground. I sat in silent prayer. It felt as though I was sitting inside one of those Christmas decorations that you shake to make the snowflakes flicker and glitter inside.

Once my breathing calmed down and my senses came back into my body, I began focusing on specific things in order to ground myself. Then, my eyes fell on something lying in the water. 'Oh my word,' I thought, 'could this really be happening?' About 30 years previously, I had been on a walk in the Hogsback forest high up on the mountains and had seen an image of a leaf lying in pine needles. I glanced away and, when I walked back to the area, I couldn't find the image again.

Now, at the Buddhist retreat was exactly the same image, except that this one was somehow more, deeper. It was everything I had ever imagined life was about. I now had the power in my hands, through the camera lens, to capture this magnificent gentle message that I had been tasked with portraying to the world.

I imagine that these leaves, captured here in *Forest Walk I, Forest Walk II and Forest Walk III*, had been lying at the bottom of the pine meadow for a very long time. They had fallen from large trees which were overhanging the dam. Initially, they would have been dark in colour, having lain in the mixture of water and pine needles, they had become a beautiful silver-white. There were only three of them, each lying in different spots in the water.

I began to wade gently through the water to where they were lying. I felt the whole forest was holding its breath, watching me as

Forest Walk III

I was about to photograph something so profound. Sometimes in life you just know all there is to know about something and some-one. This was one of those moments. It was here, in this image that all the energy of the Universe was contained.

The wise part of myself knew that this was the almighty of photographs to be photographed. It's like finding a diamond and you know it is a diamond and not a piece of glass. 'What was the meaning of this?' I asked myself.

'I know this image is filled with ancient wisdom, but what does ancient wisdom mean to me or to the world?' Maybe it was not for me to put into words at the time. Perhaps all I had to do was to take the photographs.

Oh my God, I could feel my heart race as I captured this on my camera. 'Oh my God,' I kept repeating to myself. 'How incredible is this? I am the Universe and the Universe is in me. I am this forest.' For those few moments, I felt as though I was in a trance. I had experienced something so sacred and holy and cosmic that even now I have no adequate words for any of it. I have only these images to share with the world. In those moments I realised I was not my body nor my mind nor anything else external. I was part of the make-up we call God. Was I God? Is there a difference? Or is it safer to say God was in and is in me?

I sat down on a rock overlooking the valley and thought about the experience I had just had. I was emotionally quite tired. It was a very hot, humid day, so everything felt very intense.

I wondered if the passing of my sister, Jenny, had something to do with this experience. The gift she had left me with was: 'We leave everything behind, my friends – except the part that we spend so little time with, the spirit, that lives in us.'

Yes, of course we have a body to maintain and we have to eat correctly. I've done that since becoming a vegan 20 years ago to cleanse and nourish my body. Even so, we have a commitment to the spirit world, to the Divine, to our own souls. I feel that the jour-ney for the next few years, for all of us, will be one of working our

Salute the Sun

way home; searching our souls and realising that we have to move away from power and greed onto a path that serves the planet and our own truth. If we accept that whatever is in me is also in you, then, if I am able to love all parts of my shadow self, I will allow you to experience your own life fully.

We cannot run. We cannot hide anymore. What used to work in the old days is not working anymore. I believe that we are part of a truly new age of beings who are helping to shift the world's consciousness into a space of light. This is not to say that we have to leave the darkness because, as one can see clearly in my black-and-white images, the light cannot shine without the dark. We need both.

My *Forest Walk* series shows me wrestling with my own exhaustion, my own demons, and owning them. Not blaming but embracing them. It's about me being able to dance at the top of the mountain and understand and reconnect with the deeper parts of myself, the parts that are beyond the mind, beyond the complexities of my life. It's about reconnecting with a part of me that is God. The God realisation within me is, in fact, self-realisation.

I know that I have to go down to go up and, still, while going up I am clinging to what I know. But at least I have once again caught a glimpse of who I am. I have found the strength to stay on the path journeying back home. It's a place we're all heading towards.

The *Forest Walk* series also represents the alchemist within all of us, the turning of base metal into gold. It's about understanding how our demons are in actual fact our dance partners. It's about knowing that relationships are not designed to make us happy. They are meant to make us grow.

You can either live your life in isolation up on the mountain, singing Kumbaya all day long, or you can come down off the mountain and learn to walk on hot coals in the same state of being as you attain up on the mountain. Being able to sing Kumbaya in hell takes rather more strength of character than singing it on the mountain.

Notice how we need people, things and events to constantly

New Beginning

remind us to be who we really are. The challenges almost give us permission to go within, to grow. Life itself is a self-help workshop.

Our minds are the source of our challenges. That should make the mind our enemy. In fact, because it makes us different from the animals and other elements of nature, it gives us the means to take back control in our lives. Taking back power over our thoughts, instead of simply reacting or repeating what we've been taught, gives us a diamond so bright it will light up our darkest side. It not only gives us the tool, it gives us the responsibility to make right what is broken in our lives. People cannot make us happy. It's not their job. Just like it's not our job to make our partners or friends or family happy. We are all responsible for our own happiness.

If the situation we're in is causing us to drown, then either we must gather the strength to get out of the water or we must learn to hold a longer breath. I have learned to swim underwater in my emotions and hold my breath for longer. So, I am grateful for the darkness in my life because it has helped me to realise that the people I thought loved and cared for me and didn't were doing the best they could. I don't blame them for not rescuing me. That's my job.

Understanding Love

I sometimes wake up in the mornings with a deep sadness inside of me. Tears roll down my face as I wonder if I could have done it all differently. And, if I could have, would I have?

This morning, writing these words, my tears were for a deep betrayal by someone I had absolutely believed to be my friend.

So, my question this morning is: Why does human love hurt so much whereas loving God seems to bring deep peace and inner healing? Is it because God's love is the only true love and it teaches us to disconnect from the mind?

Or perhaps we do not understand what love means. We mistake clingy, jealous love for the ultimate love. The clingy, jealous love is actually attachment and causes us tremendous pain. The more tightly we hang on to others, the more we suffer. But, we are so afraid of losing what we love, we cling on to it.

By contrast, genuine love just wants the best for the other. It does not suffocate. People come together feeling whole rather than one trying to make the other happy. We forget that each person, no matter who they are, is just someone struggling. We all long for that other in our lives, but we cannot expect that other to fill all of our holes and feelings of emptiness. We have to do that for ourselves.

I am not sorry I have loved and made a total fool of myself. I have learnt the difference between passion and power, between love and fear. I see how my growing up years and my beliefs moulded me and how I expected those around me to behave the same way as me. We seem to go through our lives finding a partner that fits our projections. Most of the time we are living in a state of illusion. The question is, are you willing to risk it all to face your own truth, no matter what? Are you able to give up wealth and security to face your core essence? Are you willing to follow your heart, no matter how and what it takes? We get so lost in who we are meant to be, the projections from our parents and society. All of this removes us from the path that will take us toward our own contentment and peace.

As I wrote these words, I glanced up and happened to look into the eyes of the feral cat, Max, who adopted me a few years ago. I felt the most profound love, understanding, and compassion coming from him. There was my beloved no-mind in action. I was able to release the hurt with the tears that streamed down my cheeks.

Max's understanding showed me once more that I am all I need. I don't need human love. Max is love. Nature is love. God is love. I am love. We are all love. When we know that, really know that, we don't need anything else.

Max went to curl himself up in the sun at the window. I thought of Eckhart Tolle saying in his book, The Power of Now, that he has 'met many Zen masters and that all of them were cats.'

On my journey, dancing through life, I have had the privilege of feeling love within and for myself. It's like opening the door on a fresh summer's morning to a cool breeze that takes over your being. You breathe and say: 'I am here. I am alive. I am in love with me. I surrender to the day and all that it brings.
I am. I am. I am.'

Winter Tree

A dance between Life and Death

It's taken a few years for me to complete this book. I've had more profound experiences and I've felt that I've been dancing between life and death.

Having held my dearest sister Jenny as she passed away, I watched on as my precious Mother, whom I have been devoted to all my life, slipped out of her physical body at the age of 91 just a few years later. As Mom took her last breath I was jolted to the realization that we are truly not here on this earth forever.

As I look back on my 57 years with my Mom there is such a flood of emotions that have allowed me to have deep realisations within myself.

If life is so fleeting what is this all about? What is it that the mystics have from the start of time been trying to teach us? Why are we, as a western culture, not learning from cultures and belief systems that are thousands of years old?

"The secret of health for both mind and body is not to mourn for the past, nor to worry about the future, but to live the present moment wisely and earnestly." Bhudda

It appears that we have mentally boxed ourselves in following a box culture in all parts of our lives. When we live in a box our hearts become narrow and so have our minds. There's no way we can think for ourselves, or expand our awareness if we stay boxed in. We don't realize that in every moment we have a choice. A choice to choose our mental, physical, emotional and spiritual well-being.

How many people do you know that question life, its meaning and actually are willing to go on a Hero's journey to find our hidden treasure? I've had many students who say they want to change, but when the going gets tough they choose to stay in their box. A box they feel safe in, yet also trapped by. It's not an easy journey to discover your true nature, but one I encourage everyone I meet to go on.

We have all lived through a global pandemic where we were clearly shown how easily humans can be controlled by using fear. Fear isolates us from one another, but more importantly from ourselves. Yet during the pandemic, all I kept hearing was people wanting to get back to normal? What is 'normal'?

For me, 'normal' is you being your true self – knowing your core essence and being yourself in all parts of your life and work. Choosing not to live in a box that someone else has defined for you. Choosing to explore all parts of who you are and looking in the mirror of the situations and circumstances and relationships that you find yourself in.

Being a normal human being is someone who loves all parts of themselves unconditionally. They love others unconditionally and they love all of nature and the teacher she is. We can't live from love if we're constantly living in fear. We have to choose one or the other.

I used to fear looking at my deepest shadows. I was embarrassed and ashamed. But it was only when I was prompted by situations, including a life-threatening illness at age 38, that I really stopped and took time to really look at myself. It's not been easy but I've had many wonderful experiences in my life. I'm so grateful. It's wonderful to have been given the gift of capturing images others don't see so that I can guide, teach and support others to explore who they are and embrace all parts of themselves with love.

The truth is we are all dancing between life and death. We are dying every moment of each day. We are in fact walking ourselves home; home back to where we came from, home back to the great spirit and the light. Surely, in this lifetime we must point our hearts, minds and spirits in the direction to which we are returning - home.

Thank you for journeying with me. I invite you to join me in the dance with life as you journey inward and upward.

**"Know your turmoil is just stuff. You are always connected to the God within. You are safe."
From my book, <u>Ebb & Flow</u>**

Marlene x
December 2022

An email from someone for whom the energy in my images has been a solace:

Hi there

Not sure if Marlene reads 'fan mail' but I really wanted to share our story with her.

In February last year my dad and step mom had sold their 10ha agricultural holding in Nietgedacht/Muldersdrift after 15 years of growing veggies, stabling horses and working hard to make a living off the land, so to speak. They loved living out of town but the crime in the area was escalating quite badly and I think they both realised that 70+ is a good age to go smaller. The farm took a few years to sell but everything seemed to fall into place when they found a small house in Sedgefield to buy. Bev was so excited she could hardly contain herself and I have no doubt my dad was too as he dealt with the practicalities of the move.

My dad has lived a life in love with the African bush and environment. As children we holidayed as far from people as possible in the still, quiet presence of the wild and thus the African landscape is very special to us.

On the Friday evening on weekend of the move (they would drive on Monday after the truck left on Sunday), my dad and Bev were attacked on their farm while they were sitting amongst the mover's boxes in their lounge at the end of an exhausting day of packing. Both were hit by bullets and by the time we had got them to hospital in different ambulances it was clear that Bev's wound was quite serious. My dad's wound was small in comparison; the bullet went through his arm near his elbow, missing all the bone/tendons etc. The bullet that penetrated Bev above her shoulder aiming downwards hit her lung, colon, and liver. The lung and colon were relatively easy to 'fix up' but the liver was so badly shattered that the bleeding parts needed to be trimmed - which meant Bev would have a very small piece of liver left to live with. That was if they could stop the bleeding so that they could operate, and then manage to keep her alive through the surgery. To cut a very long story a little shorter, Bev was in ICU for three months and lucid for only about two weeks of that time but eventually succumbed to her wounds.

This meant dad and I had a lot of time to gaze at the artwork on the walls in the Life Fourways Hospital. We were transfixed by the beauty of Marlene's photos, loving especially the aloes. We would discuss them at length and then go on trips down memory lane of all the places we had been to in South Africa (how privileged I am to have seen so much of our country). I remain convinced that the receptionists in the doctor's rooms near the photographs believed us to have a very unhealthy obsession with the images!

I had written Marlene's name on an old till slip in my bag and only actually looked at her website a few months ago. When the book arrived last week (it is my dad's Christmas present), I found myself quite moved. The brain is an amazing thing! I paged through the book and the tears just poured! My emotions came tumbling out of me and the grief overwhelmed me in a way it has not yet. But I was left with a sense of peace and I have no doubt in my mind that the photos in the hospital served my dad and I psychologically and spiritually. They assisted with trauma debriefing and allowed us quiet reflective moments in the chaos. And of course we were constantly reminded that it was from dust that we came and to the beautiful earth our bodies will all return.

I know that my dad will also find that the photographs will trigger his emotions. But I also know that they will go a long way in healing him and restoring his faith in the world.

Much love,
Nicola

Nicola Dickason
Youth Pastor @ MPC

Ready for your next step in your Dance with Life?

Get in touch through my website: marleneneumann.com

Listen in through my YouTube channel: https://www.youtube.com/@MarleneNeumann

Other books by Marlene Neumann:

Sky meets Land

Ebb and Flow

Walking Yourself Home – to be published mid 2023

Video Series: Capturing what people don't talk about

References

Wendell Berry, *Standing by Words*, North Point Press, 1986

Lewis Carroll, *Alice in Wonderland*, Macmillan, 1865

John F. Demartini, T*he Breakthrough Experience: A Revolutionary New Approach to Personal Transformation*, Hay House, 2002

Louise Hay, *You can Heal your Life*, Hay House, 1984

Jack Kornfield, *A Lamp in the Darkness*, Sounds True Inc, 2014

Caroline Myss, *Navigating Hope*, Sounds True, 2010

Marlene Neumann, *Sky meets Land*, Marlene Neumann, 2014

Marlene Neumann, *Ebb and Flow*, Marlene Neumann, 2019

Marlene Neumann, *Capturing What People Don't Talk About*, Marlene Neumann, 2016

Don Miguel Ruiz, *The Four Agreements*, Amber-Allen Publishing, 1997

Eckhart Tolle, *The Power of Now*, New World Library, 2004

Lightning Source UK Ltd.
Milton Keynes UK
UKHW050229310123
416192UK00005B/8

9 780639 755953